Robert Hamberger

Nude Against A Rock

First published in 2024
by Waterloo Press (Hove)
95 Wick Hall
Furze Hill
Hove BN3 1NG

Printed in Palatino Linotype 11pt by
One Digital
Unit 7 & 8 Woodingdean Business Park
Sea View Way
Brighton
East Sussex BN2 6NX

Robert Hamberger is hereby identified as author of this work in
accordance with Section 77 of the Copyright, Designs and Patents
Act 1988

A CIP record for this book is available from the British Library

ISBN: 978-1-915241-17-7

Acknowledgements

Grateful acknowledgements are due to the editors of the following publications, in which some of these poems, including some earlier versions, first appeared: *Acumen*; *A Scream of Many Colours* (Poetry Space Ltd, 2019); *The Cannon's Mouth*; *Christmas Together* (Candlestick Press, 2021); *Climate Matters* (Riptide Journal, 2020); *Dreich*; *Envoi*; *Everything That Can Happen* (Emma Press, 2019); *Finished Creatures*; *The Four Faced Liar*; *14 Magazine*; *Fourteen Poems*; *The Frogmore Papers*; *The Gay & Lesbian Review*; *Gutter*; *The High Window*; *Joy//Us: poems of queer joy* (Arachne Press, 2024); *The London Magazine*; *Long Poem Magazine*; *Masculinity: an anthology of modern voices* (Broken Sleep Books, 2024); *The North*; *Obsessed with Pipework*; *Poetry & All That Jazz*; *Poetry Birmingham Literary Journal*; *Poetry Salzburg Review*; *Poetry Wales*; *Raceme*; *The Rialto*; *The SHOp*; *The Spectator*; *Stand*; *Tears In The Fence*; *Words for the Wild*.

'Funny Girl' won The London Magazine Poetry Prize, 2023. 'Sleeping with uncertainty' was second runner-up in The Frogmore Poetry Prize, 2019. 'Love song for a bigot' won second place in the (Open) Oxford Brookes International Poetry Competition, 2019.

Thanks are due to Mary Allen; Clare Best; Gillie Bolton; Bernadette Cremin; Caroline Davies; Hugh Dunkerley; Naomi Foyle; Vanessa Gebbie; Maria Jastrzębska; Annie Kerr; Joanna Lowry; Simon Maddrell; John McCullough; Marian McCraith; Ann Perrin; Stuart Pickford; Catherine Smith; Janet Sutherland; Pam Thompson and Jackie Wills for their support in improving these poems. Abiding gratitude to my husband Keith Rainger for his generosity towards my writing, and for everything else.

'Playing *Love Hangover* while washing up' includes lyrics by Pamela Sawyer and Marilyn McLeod (1976) and Ralph Blane (1943). 'My husband sings' includes lyrics by Alan Jay Lerner (1956). 'Funny Girl' includes lyrics by Bob Merrill (1964). 'My aunts singing' includes lyrics by Arthur Freed (1923). 'Life's what you make it' includes lyrics by Mark Hollis (1986). The epigraph to 'Painting the fence' can be found at https://amp.theguardian.com/artanddesign/2006/may/27/art.art The epigraph to 'Anything in the world' is from *Winifred Nicholson: Music of Colour* (Kettle's Yard, University of Cambridge) page 29. The epigraph to 'First Nations man in a Montreal sauna' can be found at https://www.theguardian.com/books/2020/jul/02/natalie-diaz-postcolonial-love-poem-shortlisted-forward-prize-collection-interview The epigraph to 'A year of your life' is from *Averno* by Louise Glück (Carcanet, 2006) page 44.

The epigraphs to 'Nude Against A Rock' are from *Keith Vaughan: His Life and Work* by Malcolm Yorke (Constable and Company, London, 1990); *Keith Vaughan: Journals, 1939-1977* (Faber and Faber, London, 2010) and *Drawing To A Close: The Final Journals of Keith Vaughan*, edited by Gerard Hastings (Pagham Press, 2012). The paintings, photographs and drawings that inspired the poems can be found in *Keith Vaughan: Paintings and Drawings* (Osborne Samuel, London, 2007); *Keith Vaughan: Gouaches, Drawings & Prints* (Osborne Samuel, London, 2011); *Keith Vaughan* by Philip Vann and Gerard Hastings (Lund Humphries in association with Osborne Samuel, Farnham, 2012); *Keith Vaughan: The Mature Oils 1946-1977* by Anthony Hepworth and Ian Massey (Sansom & Company, Bristol, 2012); *Keith Vaughan: Centenary Tribute* (Osborne Samuel, London, 2012); *Keith Vaughan: The Photographs* by Gerard Hastings (Pagham Press, 2013) and *Keith Vaughan: On Pagham Beach, Photographs and Collages from the 1930s* (Austin/Desmond Fine Art, London, 2017).

By the same author:

Warpaint Angel (Blackwater Press, 1997)

The Smug Bridegroom (Five Leaves, 2002)

Torso (Redbeck Press, 2007)

Blue Wallpaper (Waterloo Press, 2019)

A Length Of Road: Finding myself in the footsteps of John Clare (John Murray, 2021)

Contents

My Husband Sings

Anything In The World

Nude Against A Rock

for
Lennox and Harrison

My Husband Sings

First day

Making love on the first day of the year
our mouths seek all the slippery places
to feast on. Our words might disappear
with a patter of kisses. Each pulse races
like a spaniel to lick the gravy.
Your fingerprints tap my skin while you
translate me by touch, as if praising me
for reading your language, solving your clue.
Pull me tighter. We make this together,
like rain persuades a pavement to accept
it's wet. This year will do whatever
it decides. We dive through minutes, adept
as older lovers meeting in a room
where my breath catches when I say your name.

Blue

When I half-wake at night and glimpse your back
by the dimmest bulb from a far streetlight
I know I'm safe at last. Tonight I lack
nothing, no-one. I should sleep easy, despite
unsettled dreams where the old fears quiver
their contours. What shadows can I see
if our duvet slips down and you shiver?
You might even turn over to face me
if your private dream allows, but for now
here's the cobalt-blue slope of your shoulder,
dark hillock of your shoulder-blade, furrow
along your spine, its cleft of lavender.
When my kiss flits your nape it won't wake you
until our room recovers the palest blue.

My husband sings

He doesn't do it often. When he does
I know he's happy. On the morning
of our wedding he's a trumpet to the tune
I'm getting married in the morning,
as we fiddle with the pins
of rose buttonholes on our lapels,
become posh versions of ourselves.
Ding-dong the bells are gonna chime.
He's a trombone now and I'm in love
with every oompah note, with that
stubble on his cheek when I kiss it,
before we say the words together
add our names to paper
and stride beside the waves as married men.

Love song for a bigot

I refuse to disappear –
          this hand is my complexity,
count its rivers and wedding rings.
Marrying a man is my victory,
your disgust. If years before I married
a woman, that proves the riches of love –
see them pour from the unpeopled heavens.
I slip like an otter past your nets.
Note how various I am – my children carry
rivers in their hands, my ancestors lifted
doors onto their backs, lifted toddlers
and boxes in their arms two hundred years
ago, tested home against the holes
in their boots, the spit of neighbours.

I come from heroines who spoke another
language – see them climb carefully
into rickety boats, measuring safety over
every wave and mile, shushing their babies,
softly patting their backs, pinning hopes
on half an hour's doze. What triumphs!
To arrive and think *I'm not welcome here
but that door needs a lick of paint. I'll make it
mine.* I carry their name and if you can't
pronounce it – if it gutters
against your tongue –
it's as glorious as my fingerprints,
singing for my mouth that shapes it,
my ear that answers to it like a perky dog.

If whatever I do tonight
makes you shudder you don't need
to watch. When I kiss his eyebrow
his shoulder his dick it's none
of your business. I claim sanctuary
in his arms. My door is bolted.
I'm an eel and he's my river.

[4]

Call me scary queen or gully queen.
Quote Leviticus, its abominations. Answer
me with your machete. *It's nothing personal.*
Stop me seeing my child, my grandchild.
I might infect them with my love. Build
a thousand walls to block me, I'll find
a thousand rivers to swim.

Gaza

We sat on the prom staring out to sea
when I read you a sonnet about Gaza.
We stayed quiet half a minute, until
you said *I fear I'll never live to see*
the end of that. You may – but I think
it'll drag on for ages. I understood
you were giving me permission for years
without you, making me fill a little life
after you've gone, hanging on
for Gaza to be solved, waiting
for no more boys to be killed
playing football on the sand.
We fell silent again, wanting Gaza
glorious and you here to see it. You. Here.

Leaving our bed

If you wake at night and leave our bed
I run my hand or foot over the sheet
where you've risen – warmed by your scent,
your absence swimming inside my head
until you return. I can sleep undisturbed
again – you're where you belong after midnight,
our darkest rendezvous, this place to meet,
the hours and sagged pillows appointed.
Can't I let you out of my sight? Being
older now (we're both older now) with your heart
on my mind, is there some way of freeing
you from my side? Letting us wake, sleep, part
whenever we please, fitfully dreaming
you'll stumble back to where I doze and wait.

All they can see

When we choose to kiss it will be in wide-awake air
    with witnesses tut-tutting at two blatant men, as if
        archangels blunted their swords, paradise failed to expel us.

We'll be accompanied by pigeons and fountains,
    tourists nibbling popcorn, water spurting from dolphins
        or the bronze lips of mermaids. Drops tickle bellies and tails.

I'll offer my mouth for an exchange of breath,
    lick of redemption, receive the flavour of whatever you ate
        (a tangerine, its zest like prickly juice that tints my tongue.)

Let me taste you – how different from me you feel, while all they can see
    is two men kissing, one shorter than the other, glasses perched
        on noses, pink carnations crinkling our neat lapels.

My husband falling

Time trips you like a pavement,
says *I'll show you what falling's for.*
It's a stony lesson – cuts to lip
and wrist and knee, where skin
meets slabs.

The solicitude of women,
a man's joke about brandy, your
younger husband lifting you,
using both hands to balance
your weight, raise you to your
feet, ensure you stand upright
again, planted in your shoes
as if falling becomes improbable,
though time might be riding to
trip you once more, chiding you
to steady yourself, slow down.

What are hands for but to save you
from falling? What are cuts for
but to show why blood travels
under your skin? See how quickly
falling proves our fragility,
precious as breath, as gold.

Snail

That snail stuck to our glass door spoils my view
of the garden. I itch to chuck it, but
you won't let me. *Don't you dare! It's got*
a right to be there – as much right as you.
I was here first, I want to argue.
Must I love its glutinous thumbprint?
This bulbous blot, glued like the stickiest
kiss on my glass, a whorled curlicue.
Do snails sleep? Is it dead already?
I pull the curtain back at night when you're
dreaming, and squint to understand. Steady
now – it's a snail. We've locked the door.
Next morning it's still there, pebble-heavy.
Tomorrow I'll swipe its smeary signature.

My husband in Venice

He clambers like a boy to the jolting prow
of the water taxi for his first lit view.

Needs a hand down the steps of The Rialto bridge –
one by careful one – fingers press its white edge.

He stirs his macchiato with precision,
a tiny stain of foam puddles his spoon.

Sways when the gondola tilts through water
while our boatman whistles, dipping the oar.

He crosses the Grand Canal to find
cloudy domes, clothes lines, a running child.

Our vaporetto passengers yell to be let off –
the passion of their outrage makes him laugh.

He takes charge of our maps and I let him,
as lights inside this water wobble and swim.

There's always laundry

A peg drops in the grass. I swear, stoop
to retrieve it while you're working quietly,
hanging up the next towel, my underpants.
I unfurl this wide pink sheet like a flag
to neighbours, if they care to notice
two men letting their daily clothes
sway in the cool embrace of air.
Here's my shirt, your paisley pyjamas.
While the virus kills outside our garden
we've agreed not to kiss, for safety's sake.
I think of Venetian washing lines,
how every morning someone's hanging out
damp socks, hoping for a touch of sun.

My husband shops in the pandemic

Go from me to buy your socks and pants.
Grab your solitude because you deserve it.
I can't always be your shield, fashioned
in the toughest bronze, some battle on my
breast, where men die bravely and horses rear
their hooves before they charge. When you say
I need a break, I presume from home and hiding.
It's not my place to hamper you, deny you streets
three metres wide of a cough. I say *Be careful –*
that's warning enough. You're alone with your
mask, out of my hands, as if your body's quick
escape slips past my fingers. Risk yourself
in a restaurant. Own your chances without my
scold. While I sit (patient, impatient) in our
kitchen's safety, you move through restless air.

My husband waits for pain to go

I find you in the dark and you explain,
looking weary on a chair, not defeated,
but paying it respect, when pain
visits. You sit and listen to its heated
argument in your skin, having paused here
before. You can't move to the other side
of hurt, until your body shifts each gear
without a thought and time's a happy ride.
Let's talk straight. Sail through the operation,
restored to yourself, and me – I'll take
what I get: wounded husband, slow motion
recovery towards another spring. Let's make
more years together, however they run,
two men holding tight in this winter sun.

My husband in hospital

I can't visit your ward. The pandemic
bars me, so we fall back on our phones.
It's your heart again, which means I panic
for your life. I mustn't be the man who moans.
Stay calm – it's not about me. I'm listening
to your voice. Does it sound breathless, anxious,
or relieved by the doctor's news, listing
good ways to get better in your gracious
syllables? I need a hug when you
say you've been hooked to a drip for six days,
six nights, to sort your blood. What's the view
from your window – is it hills, a sea-haze,
only clouds? There's so much I fail to know:
how your heart works, why we love, where years go.

New gold

You lost your wedding ring in hospital.
Your fingers thinned. It slipped somewhere.
So I'll marry you again. Right here –
while the jeweller jokes she wanted to kill
her husband after three years – I will
inch this new gold onto your third finger
left hand, over nail, ridge, joint, forever
circled. She's our witness when I say *All*
that I am I give to you as my vow.
Yours looks shinier than mine. We place
our hands together to compare, to show
how the years etch rings and skin. We face
whatever comes (old romantics, husbands now)
like the first night I found you, felt your voice.

Café Roma

How many years since we ate here – nine, ten?
We called it the smoky café before the ban,
took the kids upstairs for pasta each time
they stayed with us. Now they wake inside
their lives, miles away, and we (who feared
this place had shut) share pizza on our return:
olives dotted over cheese, as if minutes are
mushrooms, aubergines like cities we love.
Sure, the manageress behind the bar
has a subtle map of lines across her face,
though her hair-dye is red as history.
The leaning tower fades on the wall
above our forks. We're old, not wise,
savouring chips with mayo, crusts and wine.

On our anniversary of meeting
for Keith A.Rainger

Knowing you for twenty eight years makes
everything possible, dazzles at dawn.
I still whistle beside you. Who'd have thought it?
Tell each grass blade to greet rain in our garden.
Help ten goldfinches to pick sunflower seeds.
All we do is talk and listen, burnish our days.
Rare to find a man who handles me like wine
and pours us from morning towards midnight
in a double aria, like this wren answers that
nightingale, swaps notes, mixes languages,
gaining the sky as if loosened from branches,
earning more time together please, to
repair our wings, claim each other, sing again.

Anything In The World

On first looking into Alvarez's *The New Poetry*

Its cover splatters paint, the way any new
poetry should, as if stanzas could dribble
beyond paper, twist words through your ribs, trouble
your tongue, because colours might never be blue
enough to honour this sky, that sea, and you
might never touch a brush again, when you handle
this book, open as an oyster. Pages ripple
and images swim into a schoolboy's view.
Flames catch your hand when Plath calls her skin
a Nazi lampshade, Lowell speaks of a mind
not right, Sexton sings about blueberries and tin.
The walls of your art room widen. All the signed
apples, daffodils and stones flurry like each fin
of a goldfish, sycamore keys poised to unwind.

One of these mornings
for Mario

Although my mother has died
she's alive in my dream, letting me
lean against the warm rock of her side,
resting her arm round my shoulder, gently
telling me *You don't have to die.* I wake
thinking about the black drag queen who sang
a bluesy *Summertime*, that sleek
white gardenia in her hair, lifting
her voice to glory in the room. Her visa
ran out. Letters drifted. The last we heard
she flew back home to South Carolina
and hanged herself. Was she scared
no-one would tell her *You don't have to die*?
Let her rise up singing and take to the sky.

Funny Girl

On the brink of my teens at the Dominion
I watch with my mother through the black.
Omar and Barbra glow against
our faces, sing *You Are Woman,*
I Am Man in that heart-red boudoir
on a sixty-foot screen. Omar's dinner jacket,
clipped moustache, brown eyes bigger
than my head, Barbra's piled-up hair, blue
diamanté matching her fan, sway me
with their duet. I'm slinking inside their
embrace. She surrenders the swan
of her neck, shuts her lilac-shadow eyes.

Omar gathers her in his arms, croons
Does it take more explanation than this?
My mother knows who's woman who's
man, though she's still trying to be
father and mother, fill the shape of his
gap. Is this how men serenade women
who find it so absurd it makes them laugh?
I want to unbuckle their clothes,
(bow tie at the throat, blue diamanté)
unfold whoever's softer to the touch:
his hand or hers, my finger to lips,
sense (when it's night) his mouth on mine.

It's a feeling I like feeling very much.
When no-one's watching I risk being
woman and man, wriggle between their
voices, blur before their smoky gaze,
my skin a swan's feather
prickling at the wing. I burst into
flames with this feeling, all the time
sitting silent in my singed and secret dark.

A hug near The Dover Castle
for Andrew

Was it our last, or do I tell myself that?
In the street, a stone's throw from The Dover,
we readied for goodbye. Suddenly you
hugged me so tight it squeezed the breath
out of me: a tiny puff from my mouth.
Since I felt slightly astonished by its strength
I'm sorry I never hugged you back as hard.
Yes my arms wrapped round you, but it was
a 70/30 hug. Diamond friend, whom I loved
and never wholly understood, you clinched
the gift of pulling me to your chest, making those
arms (on which you worked for hours in the gym)
clasp me to your bosom in that happy moment,
resting your head on my shoulder – then gone.

The wood near Brampton Ash

Paw shadowing paw, how this pad and that
slunk through mud last night.

I can sniff out a snail,
parting dark grass to watch its triumph.

Bluebells droop their dusky memories.
I run here sometimes, mist overcoming my shins.

Rain's a messenger. Sun snips the leaf-buds,
making flames I swerve between.

Badgers and bats have left me to this breath:
a grey feather aches before my mouth.

Kneel again to the snail,
not for prayer, but for patient attention.

Ten Mother's Days

Mother's Day ten years after mum died. I'm thinking how mothers stay inside you for a lifetime, as you were – for nine months or less – inside them. Having no mothers we visit ninety-one year old Peggy in the nursing home. On my phone I show her a boat in the haze, but she can't see it because of her eyes. She's in pain more often now, and compares it to her labour with her son Clifford who died twenty-eight years ago, but perhaps the body's memory of pain never goes away. She doesn't like flowers, so we bring none. Tulips and daffodils I planted last autumn bloom in today's sun. Such flagrant pennants of red and yellow, as if the earth needs to flower whatever pain's inflicted, as if soil might be a mother, or memory a blue boat in the haze, my mother walking towards me again in her skirt of foggy roses.

Carried
for Salim Ullah, fleeing Myanmar

To be carried across this river by my son
means I give up every wish to teach him
how to lift, beg forgiveness for the burden
of myself. History steals my legs
from under me. If my head's a colander
pardon me for rain. I thought nothing
could burn my walls, lampshades, rugs
until today. Now I call to be lifted over
water, where old men are sung to sleep
by sons with bony shoulders who
remember fathers shouting. Honour me
by steeping your thighs through a river's
weather. Set me down and let us rest
like a stony answer on safe mud.

Millbeck

My silhouette climbs a twisted tree,
leaves tipping rain from open palms.

Spirals and swirls of midges agitate air.
The skin of a mountain becomes my mother's hand.

Is this how forgiveness tastes?
A robin's green shadow flickers the grass.

My kingdom's a vapour-trail
slurring a line of chalk-dust down the blue.

Knitting pattern

Why have I saved her handwriting? A lined page, pencil words:
1. Knit 5Main 5Navy 26Main 2Green 4Main 6Grn 5Main
I don't know the code, but she knew. Now her ashes sift
where minnows open mouths and water moves above her.
I can't understand that either. It's her message.
2. Purl 4Main 9Grn 2Main 2Gr 24Main 10Navy 2Main
I don't know how to stitch one colour after the other,
add one word to the next, though I persevere,
a pencil over this page the sign of her hand once
moving. I want her to be in the air again, beside me
knitting or talking. I won't look away this time, her
needles clicking like minutes. *1Main 12Navy 23Main*

Perrett's Park

I laze in honey air, eyes closing.
Light heats my skin. I tune into birdsong,
trying to guess if it's a linnet dousing
this hour with those notes. I may be wrong.
I give up and allow leaf shadow
to patter my face, let myself drift
through minutes, forget where I am, allow
a sense of grass and my body to sift
enough breath together to bring me calm.
This could be consolation. I might even
stay forever, since there's no harm
in birdsong looping its language, no reason
to lift a hand or stretch a muscle,
losing myself in the sky, lying still.

Rain in Istanbul

She tells me *There's rain in Istanbul,*
so I buy an umbrella for my daughter
the day before she flies again. I figure
black with small pink butterflies will
open beautifully outside the hotel,
each splash fizzling like the wettest fire.
She says *I want to go everywhere.*
My fear can't clip her wings. May this frail
umbrella shelter her from harm
in Paris, New York, Honduras, Thailand.
My undaunted daughter flies safely home
five days later. Rain fell outside the Grand
Bazaar, the Blue Mosque, the Baths where a balm
of water dropped soft coins into her hand.

Father Quartet
for Alf Hamberger

A month before

A month before my father died he said
Close the curtains and shut the door. He made up
his mind he didn't need any more world.
What honey had it offered to his lip?
They carried his bed downstairs. He was King
Lear in the front room: sunk cheeks, snow beard,
pigeon chest, the trees of his hands. Eating
hassled his tongue, as though taste bored
him now. While leaves spun from their
October branches, sparrows tussled
in gutters, he asked me not to share
the sun with him. Uncertain, troubled,
I drew those curtains but left a gap, as though
to pierce him with light when he wanted shadow.

My father dying

His mouth's a small pit
for air to fall inside, his dull blue
eyes half open, so I mistake – for a split
second – his sleep for waking. I never knew
how much could be stripped from him and still
keep him as my father, though I scour
the missing years for something to fill
my heart. Even if I wait another hour
I'll fail to wake him. This sleep has broken
him from me. These breaths. His hand on his chest,
its swell and drop. My name should be spoken
before I kiss his forehead, as if it's best
for me to go gently, to leave him
songs from the radio skimming his room.

To throw a rose

Who knew a rose would bounce on a coffin
when dropped, as farewell, from such a height?
I feel grateful to the aunt not seen
for years, who lets me rest my head's weight
on her shoulder and cry like a lost boy.
Those years of never knowing him swoop back.
She mothers me until my face is dry,
him lying in earth below me. Might the lack
I carry become an absence? Let that tree
nearby, its ravaged bark, shelter him
next spring, flickering a thousand leaves, free
as air above him. When we drive home,
rising from the tunnel, a double rainbow
fades to cloud, as if saying *let him go.*

Five weeks after

Even a cat can teach a tough lesson.
She stops eating five weeks after
my father died. They never knew each other,
so why, when I lift her weakness – frail bone
and fur – am I lifting him, and why, when
we make that grey decision, does my father,
his disappearance, flood the room? We stroke her
gently as the vet eases sleek poison
into her. I hold her head, while she
stares at me with witch-hazel
eyes; then she's gone. The flat sounds empty
when we come home. I'm thankful
their pain is over, but the day's more lonely
with one less cat or father, the night more chill.

Painting the fence

It is the business of a painter not to contend with nature and put this scene on a canvas of a few inches, but to make something out of nothing, in attempting which he must almost of necessity become poetical.

John Constable, Letter to John Fisher, 24th August 1824

It's *Seagrass* – or it will be, if I can
paint the damn thing right. Woodlice creep out
above my brush, think better of it,
retreat. A spider walks her invisible line.
I say sorry when I flick her away, gone
into the air. All that handiwork! I devote
hours to seagrass. Each stroke down each slat
soothes the wood, as if knots might be undone,
finds me making something out of nothing
where goldfinches nip at sunflower seeds
and clouds withhold their rain. I'm standing
on newspaper among drops. My wrist needs
this rhythm of dip and brush, stepping
back to check my work while a sparrow feeds.

Street song

I keep walking – my collar's corner
an edge of folded paper. I refuse
the wren's burden on a branch, its noose
of notes the nearest thing to a mother
on cold mornings, though I'm brighter
than this streetlamp, rosier than a bruise
on linen skin. Who owns me? Who chose
to call me mister when time's harder
than ten pavements and I need no sparrows
whistling for my crumbs? That moon's a smoky
halo from last night. No skinny dog follows
me. If you want to eat my story
I won't give you the pleasure. Tomorrow's
another road. Its puddles sing to me.

Queens

Dragging ourselves past man-traps, straitjackets,
cages, we've been good boys walking in straight
lines. We bend the rules now, balance on stilettos,
dent our shame into shape. Snorting like unbroken
stallions, let's wallow in girly songs, mouthing
every word – let's pirouette under cherry trees,
squint through keyholes at a showering man,
because we understand why that mongrel sniffs
each lamppost. Let's not go meekly to the
knacker's yard. Next winter let's be nimble
queens climbing horse chestnuts, swinging,
sawing, shouting down, while our branches
drop on pavements like a messy nest, as if
we must be cut before we can blossom.

My aunts singing

At the fag end of parties, when the dregs
have been drunk. Songs like *Who's sorry now?*
Such resignation in five voices begs
for understanding, for love to treat them how
they deserve, with kindness, a touch of sympathy
for the hard graft of their days, their disillusion
past midnight in this crowded room, when tea
should be their last drink – or another gin
and lemon for the road, for old times' sake.
They're moving onto *I cried for you,*
now it's your turn to cry over me. They make
each other sway to the tune, a slow blue
melancholy more comforting than men,
while my uncles flick ash, don't join in.

3am break-in

If a window is smashed it's because
the one outside wants in,
wants whatever inside has
that outside has not.

Could a membrane between
less and more call to be broken,
for a curtain to be swept aside
to claim whatever they can grab?

Inside, a scream
alerts outside that broken glass
means injury – *this is my home,*
my sacred space stormed, withheld.

Scream makes the dispossessed one
run past potted roses, lilac,
where night remains
unwelcoming, without.

My mother ironing

She taught me the best way to iron a shirt
and I follow her faithfully: easing
along the collar, nudging across each hurt
and crumpled sleeve, the pleats uncreasing
while my hand glides to smooth both cuffs,
as if this iron might solve every buttonhole,
calm those puckered stitches. Heat buffs
its prow over rucked material.
What kind of father am I? My kids sewn
into their years – did I show them how
to iron or was it something left undone?
I stand at the ironing board and don't know
what to do, except hang another
shirt in a room emptied of my mother.

Madison Square Park on July 14th

A shaven-haired man in a blue T-shirt talks to the phone in his ear:
Well a poem is – he weaves fast through dawdling people, so I can't
hear the rest. What's a poem – will I ever catch it? Sparrows flurry
belly feathers in the dust. A hippy-ish woman comes to my bench
and asks *Sir, do you have any pain in your body?* I say *No, I'm lucky* and
her younger male companion, bearded like Jesus, smiles and says *A
surprising number of people have no pain today.* It's my last afternoon
in New York. I must read more Frank O'Hara. As it's gone three,
Frank would have finished his lunch by now and strolled back to
the gallery. The fountain splashes into three black metal basins. It
settles and never settles, pouring endlessly in the sun. Each spurt
of water looks white this afternoon, sprinkling against scaffolding
and three black basins, palm leaves drenched in pots so they're the
lushest green, drinking whatever the fountain needs to give.

Life's what you make it
for Mark Hollis

Today, late afternoon, I play your songs.
It's how I remember – music our brightest bulb.
Neighbours along the corridor on campus,
our first year. One afternoon you asked me
to your room, spun records: The Small Faces,
Them, white boys wanting to sound black.
We couldn't sniff punk spitting round the corner,
so where might moody lads hunch their edges?
You tested me, an obscure track. I recognised
his voice: *The Troggs.* You looked impressed –
but overtures faded. Maybe I seemed too tame.

Me – the good boy – falling
in love with my children's mother, though I
couldn't foresee that life. You – lank blond hair,
skinny black jeans – dating a girl who swapped
her name from Felicity to Flick, chopped her curls,
donned a leather jacket, cool with kohl eyes.

Five years later I'm in a taxi in London,
notice you (maybe Flick's beside you)
on the kerb – a guitar case weights your hand.
Are you hustling to make music, build a band,
a name? Do songs throb your hours like heartbeats?
I've married my children's mother (no kids yet)
moved to what I thought a safe space
miles from London: our honeymoon home.

Fast-forward and I'm changing my baby
on a primrose Chinese rug with swags
and pink blossom, look up at Top of the Pops
and it's you singing *Life's What You Make It* –
banging a keyboard, floppy fringe, black glasses.
I can't see your eyes. How must it feel to marry
success, everyone chanting your rhymes,
dancing to your tune, Talk Talk of the town?
Celebrate it – Don't backdate it – Nothing
can change it. Are we both *yesterday's favourite?*

Thirty years later, after I heard you died,
I read how you gave up performing to be
a father. Driving home from my kids
a hundred and sixty miles away, I play
your old hits – a man I knew, aiming
to become a better dad, burning bridges,
stardom in flames.

My husband dozes beside me.
We spin through swift dark. I turn up
your chorus, not to wake him
but to understand why life's what we make it.
Me – hours apart from my kids, facing
my desires, hoping to change the shape of love.
You – stopping your songs to lift your kids
into the air, to stay where they wake,
squabble, eat, habitual as wallpaper, music
shaking their rooms whenever it matters.

This afternoon I play your last album,
the one that simply carries your name.
What might you be teaching me, Mark?
Let the voice you're born with
be scissors, paper, stone, *the colour
of spring*. Young men coincide, move on,
perhaps grow wiser. When one of us dies –
leaves clarinets, piano chords, guitar strums –
your final notes (gull cry or love song)
soar towards silence.

Text

Love you Dad. Sorry
about your car troubles
and that we missed
seeing you. Hope
going back to work
hasn't been too much
of a drag.
The nights he wouldn't
sleep, those first three
years, I felt so spun to
the edge of myself
sometimes my temper
broke. After I smacked
I'd pat his back through
cot bars, read my bleary
book, and inch, cross-
legged, across the carpet
– slowly, slowly – not
to wake him.
Whenever my temper
broke, I woke ashamed,
and when I opened his
curtains next morning
he'd say *We love each*
other, don't we? I'm
still lit up by his words
and catch twelve seconds
from my job to press my
own words here, between
400 emails, add a kiss to
bless the man who strokes
my temple with his thumb.

Torch song

The cathedral's burning while a wren
sings *my house is on fire my children
are gone.* No – it's a ladybird singing.
She falls on her back, legs kicking –
a polar bear's ribs poke like broken
umbrellas. Twelve minutes from my
house I walk the hill where I hear
a wren babble like water, watch it
(the size of a leaf) flick between
branches. They're in danger
(this hill, that wren, those branches).
The bluebell is blackening. An ice floe
shrinks till my boots soak in a petrol
puddle. The spire wavers, topples,
but the golden cockerel's saved
– surely that counts for something
when we kneel and sing on stones,
roll helpless on our backs
air scorching our O-gaped mouths.

A son's broken nose

I fail to be there, stop the other man,
refute – with my hands if necessary –
that gargoyle male:
               his scales
               his armour
               his headbutt
      Cease!   *I'm bigger than you*
and bigger must make blood, his only
avenue, not words or hushed forgiveness,
merely *you want some?*
                    my son, the peaceful
one, raised by us to reconcile, if he can,
whether street or supermarket aisle,
stands astonished by zero to psycho
in six seconds,
          blood down his shirt,
such petals spattered like a rose –
I might have barred
          forbidden
          stood in front
to shield him, not countenance
one splash of precious –
                 wanting none,
no man to drop another, no solving this
by blood –
          my son, one month into his own
exhausted fatherhood,
          saying with me
               you will not hurt my son.

Sleeping with uncertainty

You sleep with uncertainty – that familiar
companion – never guessing when he'll go.
You doze on tenterhooks. Your pillows know
his coming or going is the breath of a liar
who'll promise mud is cloud and water's fire.
If he mentions surgery and chemo
they're possibilities he must point out, though
your biopsy will speak the body's answer.
Meanwhile his avalanche hangs above
your head. You can get through weeks this way,
rearranging spoons or those jars you love
until sun strikes him on your brightest day.
Home again – after good news – you move
to open windows, grateful for grass, for sky.

Anything in the world
for Ithamar

*I don't want anything in the world – I just like existing every minute, and
watching things coming and things going*

Winifred Nicholson, Letter to E.Jenkinson, 1925

Each minute dives too deeply to forsake.
Take the sea, for example, this morning:
its blue-grey rise from dip to whitened break –
how can I explain it? Take the meaning
of your face when I turn up every month
to play: *Who is this man?* We've got a tractor
to pile with bananas, the grinning mouth
of that pull-along crocodile, your tiger
to stroke, and with each toy I get to know
you a little more, until the minutes
become a few hours. It's time to go.
Your weariness means this strange man lifts
you in his arms before he disappears,
coming and going like waves minutes years.

At the Italian café in Totterdown

Seven diners easy with each other:
my husband at the head of the table,
my ex-wife beside me, two of our adult kids,
our daughter-in-law tilts the baby's bottle
while our grand-daughter sucks her straw.
Give them tulips. Grief's already happened.
Men lying with men are never welcome
to those who won't break bread at this table,
though I hear God is love, apparently,
because sudden happiness stirs our spoons.
How succulent these courgette slices look –
as if parmesan and pasta plug a gap.
Cucumber chunks forked from my plate
glisten on our grand-daughter's tongue.

Glisten. On our grand-daughter's tongue
cucumber chunks forked from my plate,
as if parmesan and pasta plug a gap –
how succulent these courgette slices look
because sudden happiness stirs our spoons.
Though I hear God is love, apparently
to those who won't break bread at this table
men lying with men are never welcome.
Give them tulips. Grief's already happened.
While our grand-daughter sucks her straw
our daughter-in-law tilts the baby's bottle,
my ex-wife beside me, two of our adult kids,
my husband at the head of the table –
seven diners easy with each other.

Breadcrumbs

Scooping breadcrumbs from the worktop
into my cupped hand, I think of my mother
moving her hands in her cramped kitchen
years ago. What were her thoughts
about life at any given moment collecting
crumbs? There's so much I never dreamt
to ask, consumed by my rich days,
how important my feelings seemed to me
when she was merely a room away.
I could have walked in, waited
as she worked, said *What can I do*
to make things better? I catch my
breadcrumbs, bin them, shut the lid.

First Nations man in a Montreal sauna

Can we create these intimate spaces within the very nation that doesn't want us?
                    Natalie Diaz, *The Guardian Review*, 4th July 2020

This mirror's darkness unravels our limbs
giving and taking the gifts we both crave –
fingers wallow through his thick black hair –
our living skin (he calls mine soft)
the feelings mouths engender –
more minutes overwhelming *my God*
my God wrenching from my throat.
Afterwards when we talk
in that dim intimacy he speaks
about wanting to see London
one day, and how living in his flat
is *okay most of the time* (meaning
sometimes it's not) and how he must
get back for his dinner shift at the café.

Half a cup

He asks for the price of a cup of tea.
I fish in my pocket. A pound
should cover it, though I admit secretly
it'll barely fill half a cup. He must find
more money, to please himself for an hour.
When I finger the hard edges between
two pounds and one, why do I hand over
less than he needs? Possessions glint in
me, guarded, safe. What does an extra quid
weigh in my wallet? He thanks me, calls me
sir before we part, as if such gratitude
for a pittance sends him off happily.
I jingle cash because I can,
hearing the shiny clink of each loose coin.

Golden bomber jacket

You left your golden bomber jacket in my car. We were walking through clear streets under trees. I was telling you about my ninety poems. We came to a garden where I introduced you to my new friend, while she was tying back stems, pruning roses. After we chatted and left her you said *She's beautiful.* We ran towards more roses, pulling their blowsy faces close to ours. We jumped on a bed on the lawn, laughing with children we'd never met before. When we sat in the crowded café you excused yourself to pop to the toilet. We hadn't ordered, so I waited for you. I waited for several minutes, while families chatted and ate their strawberry tarts. I waited until it dawned on me that you wouldn't be coming back, because you died thirty years ago.

Salt and blackberries
for Nita and Annie

After Nita dies I add her to my list –
walk through sea spray – lick this grit of salt
off my lips. Counting those I've lost
I run out of fingers. Their names halt
my heart, though it's still jolting. My doctor says
I've a thirteen percent chance of a stroke
or heart attack. It should be lower. Follow ways
to narrow my odds: drop dairy – take
statins – medium to high-intensity
swims, workouts, hills. My answer is to meet
Annie for blackberrying, where we see
quince, damsons, brambles, pluck these sweet
bristly globes – ripe, over-ripe – till our nails stain
like wine. Taste one more. Gorge ourselves again.

Red door

When I told my mother she must go
into a home she said *I'll die then!*
as if her threat proved all she had
to bargain with was death.
The walls we'd stolen from her
tumbled past her cheek.
Her words couldn't link
to each other, though she understood
we were making her an old woman
in a home of old women who lost
their sons' names, but thought
those heads wore noses and ears
of boys who once jutted against
her hip, like jugs at a well –
cracking now into monstrous men who
make her forget she chose wallpaper,
painted ceilings.
       Did I say *Mother,
don't die*? A laugh knocked itself
out of me, as if I'd bandaged
our burns, strapping her wrists
to her sides, so she wouldn't fly
over the park that bruised her orchid,
tarnished her necklace, buried
the keys to her flat, a red door
we found open most evenings
when the lake had swallowed her swans.

For my daughter with Covid

Honour your breathlessness. Each lung bears
its sorry dust bag in and out, while slack
devotion is entering your mouth. The knack
your body knows of getting through hours
to make you stronger. The way those fevers
flare and lapse, as if you're swaying back
and forth with air, like breathing, that hack
from coughs, your headaches. This virus wears
your white dressing-gown, takes to your bed.
Our video chats might help you thrive,
recover miles away, like the time we said
daffodils, soup and Netflix could revive
your days, keep you safe, as if we respected
how every breath's a promise to survive.

Who do we not save?
written on 10 Downing Street's whiteboard, 13th March 2020

Let's not save Peggy. She's 92,
spends too many hours in bed
watching trees through her window.
A drain on resources. Underlying
conditions. Ashok can go – granted,
he keeps the care home running,
a family man, but frankly, the wrong
accent, colour. Shall we throw
Sharon under the bus? She's an angel
on the ward, an enormous loss, so
we'll clap her away. Every life a source
of undying regret, but can we please
level up now, move on, stop carping,
build back better?

A year of your life

To what would you lose a year of your life?

Louise Glück (from *Landscape*)

As two women (one old, one young)
led their brown and white horses
down a chalky path between trees,
the white horse glanced at me
with brief curiosity from behind white
eyelashes, until it clopped past and could
notice all the leaves again.

Year of repetitions,
the sea's abiding company. An older
woman, wearing daily scarves the colour
of waves, begins to acknowledge us
late every morning, to share mild words
about the sky, how long this might last.

My year's seen daffodils, persistent
dandelions, this morning's winter
jasmine in rain, my grandson typing
his first email to say *I love you so much.*
No day is lost – perseverance: a horse
through autumn trees, sniffing
the scent of fields.

St James's Street, Brighton

You, lemon sorbet. Me, salted caramel. After chilling our tongues on gelati at La Mucca Nera – our little corner of Italy – we treat ourselves to lunch at Yelken, the new Turkish café. There are wildfires in Greece and Australia. We watch the street unwind from our table by the big window: roofers working on the Post Office opposite, five stories of scaffolding. An assured young man in a black T-shirt with his earring, sleeve of tattoos, face like a Caravaggio, stacks two handfuls of terracotta tiles into a yellow plastic bucket, which he hauls up on a rope to a shaven-headed man in his fifties, five planks above. I say *This way of hoisting tiles would have happened in Pompeii*. Two electric buggies edge past the poles on the pavement. A Deliveroo driver leaves the Black Sheep next door as a Just Eat driver enters. Are we the new Pompeii, on the brink? An old man loaded with shopping laughs that he'll climb the scaffolding. Me, stuffed vine leaves. You, grilled aubergine.

After the grandkids leave

Yes I'm a wet dishrag, but let me be
wrung out by four cries again. Eight days
isn't enough. Is my life this free,
this quiet, without them? Every room says
Where are they? as I unpeel pillowcases,
strip sheets, with no-one to interrupt,
no shout or song, no squabbles or races
down the hall, no call to be carried, to erupt
into my arms, and when they're lifted
how the years swing back: that sleepy
squirmy weight of my kids has shifted
against my chest. I'll carry them home. We
might make it right this time – no guilt, no
mistakes. I'll wash the bedclothes tomorrow.

Yellow bowl
for Nikki

It broke in two. There's no need for gold
to fix it. Clear glue and my hands
shaped like a bowl to keep it steady.

Five minutes of firm holding
might solve my invisible task.
Watch me cup my palms

around the glaze, as if moulding
a smooth nest. It can't look
good as new, yet becomes

a yellow bowl on the table once more,
staking its claim in our house of repairs.
One black hair across its slope,

centre, rim – proof of damage,
proof of being made whole again
like a man, after many years, this mended life.

Floods

Can you trust your roof,
                              that downpipe unhinged
by storms when rain refused to stop, until
you're washed away like a bed, suitcase, friend?

Our breath overtaken by water –
death in an open mouth.
                              The only thing
we managed to save is our lives.

Draw a circle of fire around yourself,
                              pray the floorboards dry again –
swear it never happens here. You're safe as flames.

I heard a man on a rescue boat:
                              My friend died
moments before you arrived. He slipped
and was swept away.

Winter Solstice
for Clifford
who would have been sixty-six

Your birthday is the briefest day,
this year free from icicles, missed by snow.

I catch echoes of your voice, my winter
jasmine. I'm a chilly friend scooping leaves.

Your jokes never lit this garden, where love
returns like a sparrowhawk scenting blood.

We're old news. It's my half of the story,
as if I'm knee-deep in memory's roses.

I might still shout your name across this evening's
early blue, without the faintest hope of your reply.

Advice to my poems

Build a harebell's fortitude in your lines.
Practise a sparrow's jab, a puddle's brink,

your pavements transfigured by rain.
Limelight's over-rated. Silence

has its uses, calm as grass.
Get your stanzas dirty. Run your nail

along that gutter – find a tattered leaf,
elastic band, dropped glove. These are

worthy of attention, like water
plunging itself, lucid over stones.

Skylarks in January

Yesterday a murder
of crows ganged up
to scare a buzzard.

This morning I lift
my eyes to song:
three skylarks

twiddling notes thirty feet
over gorse and hills.
Small commotion of wings

      hovering
precisely where they please:
three sparks under cloud,

cinders saved from the fire
– falling, falling.
What do I know?

Three quick smudges
barely higher than grass
settle, like the end of song.

The house of my body

There's a hole in the roof where pigeons
roost with rain. I ache in my rafters,
creak through joists.
Who owns these spider-hammocks
crying out not to be disturbed?
Let them go about their business
(hunger, weaving, murder) while I'm
opening doors for my years.

In the bed of my breath
friends who died thirty years ago
speak large as life, and waking becomes
a muted disappointment. My windows
shake their weathers outside. I marry
a dog to the lamppost, a pillar box
to scattering twigs, sweep my yard
of fag ends, moss clots, bus tickets.

I garden the suck and shovel
of my dirt, grub through soil
where yellow returns like morning,
scarlet also, such flags against
surrender to my neighbours the slugs.
I say *nibble little*. I say *leaf and water
and flourish*. Celebrate my blossom,
achieve my grass, give steadfast
permission to my worms.

Swan

My book's a mute swan in winter –
a hundred blank pages
soaring through glass.

Ice feathers might break
a man's arm. Call myself
dogsbody, swan

it's still the same racket.
What a clatter
stanzas make along that shelf!

Swans sail across bookshops
and libraries, forgetting
who caught or penned them.

My shifty hand nips
sixty words from the snow.

Snow church

I enter that church tonight,
so cold the stained glass

has become Paul Klee's windows,
each jade or claret square opaque with snow.

I open the second white door,
venture further inside this frost chapel,

move deeper with every chill step
until the choir upstairs falls silent.

Stone walls stand caked around me,
furred from outside, as if I'm breathing ice.

Later, when I look back on where I've been –
where I walked through those winter chambers –

each candle flame's gone like the snow.

Playing *Love Hangover* **while washing up**
for Ava

If there's a cure for this –
I'm steeping my wrists in bubbles tonight,
a twentieth century girl
reeling to seventies disco, when Diana
swoops her crazy laugh.
This first Christmas without Helen
I could work out how she might endure.

In a pewter snowflake
dangling from a tree, in the heads
of friends, or that parallel moment
when she drags on a fag and it never ends.
I could welcome my grand-daughter, a month
into her first breaths. What might I promise
Ava? She'll find giraffes and pomegranates,
cafés and politicians, damaged magnolias,
floods and forest fires, make friends who could
last nearly a lifetime.

Before I dipped these saucepans
I looped two red ribbons and two grey snowflakes
over a fir tree's bristles, thinking *one for each
lost friend*, sipping sherry, hearing Judy sing
we'll have to muddle through somehow, as if
muddling becomes its own answer.
Go Judy and Diana – give me longing
between the branches, soapsuds after
the sherry, a clatter of forks, when I rinse
once more the innocent face of a plate.

If there's a cure for this I don't want it –
my missing quartet of friends, my grand-daughter
dreaming, my twenty-first century girl.
How can I hold them all in my hands
without overflowing, while a cat laps
urgently at water, and rain tonight

wrestles away from the sea? Let it fall
like a fork or snowflake:
this unfinished welcome, this swirling song.

Nude Against A Rock

poems after Keith Vaughan

As society becomes more cramping so the art of individuals burns with a brighter and more feverish flame.

Keith Vaughan
Journals, 4th March 1944

Keith Vaughan (1912-1977) was a gay Neo-Romantic painter whose work mainly focused on the male nude and landscape. He kept a Journal from 1939 until his death. In 1966 Vaughan published edited extracts from his Journals, and in 1989 and 2012 further extracts were published.

Two figures embracing

I want more than anything someone I can love and trust and who is willing to return the same. But I cannot find that person, nor do I know any longer where to look for him.

Journals, 25th August 1939 (first entry)

A street in Amiens
where the men hunch their shoulders
and ask for a light.

A whitewashed chapel on Santorini
where I catch his eye: that glint
the tiniest flame.

Some flicker of interest – dark lashes
letting me in. (O dive, dive!)
This chill, its risk, goosepimple temptation.

To the Black Horse in Soho,
through parks at dusk, amusement arcades,
the Gents under the clock tower.

A week before war, my prince
won't come. Where's a moth meant
to settle these days, these urgent nights?

Near marble skin at the Tate
chalk and charcoal make
my paper bridegroom.

Let me say *I do*, pledge
– with head and hand –
my years to him.

Len eating a melon
(photograph on Pagham beach, summer 1939)

...his arms finished at the wrists in two logs of yellow stained wool and bandage. His right leg was a shapeless embalment of bandage...Pain too long endured bent him backwards like a strung bow, fretting his face with sweat.

Journals, 19th June 1940

Last summer
my nude stood easy in the sun,
(that shush of tide, blue after blue)
absorbed by a half-moon slice,
the prospect of taste so close
one succulent drop
quivered at his fingernail.

Tonight I tend a soldier from Dunkirk,
wanting to soothe his wounds
like a steady mother. Midnight's damage
howls fissures into skin – pulpy flesh
looped by bandages where his hands should be.
I can't sew a stitch – his wrists blunt logs,
his thigh a dingy yellow hidden from the sun.

I'm unable to mend – the beach man
careless for any juice to smear his chin,
the bandaged man stained beyond repair –
their glorious bodies singing *live, live.*
I staunch his blots, keep dabbing, mopping
while my young man smiles softly above
a melon, eager to bite.

Lazarus

We took leave of each other at the entrance to Trafalgar Square tube station. A casual wave of the hand and a smiling glance was all the ceremony...four days later he was dead.

Journals, 15th August 1940

My brother is rising again
between lions and fountains –
a quiet man dazed by pigeons.

He's hauling himself free
from wreckage, onto pavements
in the air's cool relief.

Water spills from the bronze snouts
of dolphins, while summer crowds
elbow around him, as if breathing

were the simplest act. Ice-blue
linen loosens at his shoulder,
unravels, trails like a scarf.

Might he feel reluctance to return?
Pigeons scatter – a blather of wings,
bellies and beaks. He sways

among them, source of their flight,
each bird's confusion a panicky feather
that ascends, like his breath, into sky.

Being beauteous
(after Rimbaud's *Illuminations*)

Against the folding of another nakedness in one's own no code, no
morality, no doctrine has any power at all.

Journals, 26th December 1944

Unfolding like paper, I raise my arms
one moment before embrace,
as if surrendering to the possibility
of fire, honouring each body's
dents and blemishes – beach of your
shoulder, embankment of my thigh.

Harbour me tonight, allow me inside
(wreck though I may be)
each fallible touch a foxglove
open for every bee, porous as sand
when water seeps, darkening
a thousand grains.

Nothing's holier. If I ask your name
it's all I know – that and how
you kiss. Kneel and take more into
my mouth, being animal, fluid, skin.

Floating boy
(photograph on Pagham beach, 1930s)

*Today I went to the river and the sun…and took off my clothes…I lay
back and stretched myself into the brilliant warmth. Years have passed
since I last did this. Perhaps I am the last person in Europe who can still
lie in the sun.*

Journals, 7th May 1945

Where are you lad?
                Have you survived
the war? Your face a drowsy island above
           shallow water, half-smiling,
                with salt-matted hair.
Waves lullaby,
       and below wet shoulders
pebbles may become your bed.
            Let's float our years away –
challenge the sun by lazing under it
       as if we might cheat grief this easily,
as if one summer's burn   marks us for life.

Adam

With a sudden violent agitation of the leaves, like the scattering of a tray of jewels, someone is reaching up to gather a low hanging fruit.

from 'Statement on Painting', 1951

Adam lifts his hand to pluck that fruit,
pricks his finger – flinches – slinks away.

I shape him naked as a silver birch,
breathe life into his nostrils.

The bark becomes his skin, his belly the trunk –
this outstretched arm a loaded branch.

I trace the flourish of his spine, wanting him
to twist and eat, not dip his neck, not cower.

A man, to the tips of his leaves – shall I fall
with him onto grass in our echoing garden?

Bather taking off a shirt

I ask myself which of my pictures would I be willing to stand beside in public, say Piccadilly Circus, for all to see...The continual use of the male figure...retains always the stain of a homosexual conception...I feel I must hide my head in shame.

Journals, 22nd December 1953

This bather has lost his head –
      his crooked neck disappears
inside a shirt (one sleeve dangling)
      such struggles to unwrap himself,
elbowing out of buttonholes
      to be naked as sky.

Escape artist – his knee flexes
      with effort, as if the petty
bandages of day hold him hostage,
      cuff his wrists. Once he's freed
from collars, sprung from the man-trap,
      he sprints towards slippery blue.

      Slash the nets –
kick at last against a blurred horizon.
      Let water stain his pores,
dribble through fingers
      spout from his mouth –
each splash rejoicing.

Nude against a rock

These compositions rely on the assumption (hard to justify perhaps, but none the less real to me) that the human figure, the nude, is still a valid symbol for the expression of man's aspirations and reactions to the life of his time.

from 'Painter's Progress', August 1958

When I stand my nude against a rock,
who wins? The nude scores on softness,
sleek as a man able to be gentle,
worthy of love. If his hand rests
to steady himself beside the black
bulk, it doesn't mean he believes
stone is stronger than skin, armour
the toughest way to survive.

I pitch the body against
blocks, boulders and monoliths
somewhere near the sea, under
pewter cloud. What a weight he carries
on his shoulders! This gilt sun
travels across his nipples, torso, groin,
glinting patches of pistachio and coral,
even pearl.

I'll balance my final touches
with a truce – each leaning on the other.
That crag cushions his shoulder
when he tilts his chin.
Shadows cross-hatch their stony valley.
This man rises like a vulnerable answer
always saying yes.

Figures in a bar

I could have won one of the waiting ones & brought him home, but then all I wanted would vanish, the fantasy. So I watch & watch the watchers who watch me & wonder.

Journals, 11th November 1961

Hemmed in by half-drunk
pints, our furtive glances,
my night watch

for your lips and eyebrows
makes me itch to lick
that puddle under your glass.

The courage to strike a match,
to act or step back.
Close-ups in my head

follow me home.
I'll ink your smoky ghost
across my sheets.

Red assembly

Remarkable experience to visit this place where homosexuality is natural,
accepted & expressed...How sensible of the Dutch. One wants to clap...
Couples dancing – some well – some badly – but all a sort of dream-like
tenderness – clasping and kissing.

Journals, 31ˢᵗ October 1963 (Amsterdam)

A red assembly sways under dusky sky –
what music called us here, drew us together?

That pierce of joy – dress in it, embody it
tonight. Drag on a fag to order it at the bar.

Spin me as far as your arm, then pull me close –
every wave resists before it topples.

Dance until sweat peppers with dew – the friction
of caress, rubbing shoulders, breath flickers breath.

Our scrum wrestles naked from useless clothes –
hallelujah burnishing our throats.

Saint Sebastian (Johnny Walsh)

Extraordinary night with Johnny Walsh…The whipping was exciting to
start with. He co-operated with the idea straight away as a way of atoning
for his sinful ways.

Journals, 22nd December 1963

I cottoned on quick how queers have
the hots for me. I glow under their kisses
like coal. He draws & paints & whips
me, begs me to tan his hide. I pocket
his dosh for stripping – electric shocks –

our secret games. My tarts, my effing
& blinding, tinkle his cut-glass laugh.
Posh art boils down to this – stings
& bruises. When he hurts he reckons
it'll wash my sinful ways.

It's easy money – but this one
niggles inside my tattoos. I want
to please him. He tells me to lift
my elbows, blabs about a saint
shot by arrows – a stuck pig.

Any room for sissy-softness?
Lick my armpits.
I'm his filthy angel –
pure as the driven.
His arrows zing the air & spike my skin.

Winter landscape (Gladys Vaughan)

Sad at 50 that I still cannot get beyond a suppressed matriarchal loathing and contempt for the selfishness (which I inherit) and self-centred dogged energy and drive of that woman.

Journals, 8th March 1964

I'm not only *his* mother. My younger son
died, his plane shot down. In dreams I see him
hurtling through the sky. I've no grandchildren,
few blessings. My convent school in Belgium
haunts me still, packed off as a girl when I was
in their way. I played the violin wonderfully.
Now it's frozen, locked. My husband left us
when the boys were small. My son hates me,
says I fuss, wring him dry, my love swallows
him whole. I carry every disappointment,
tidy my days, hang on until he allows
me to see him – then sun makes the snow melt.
Winter scares me, numbing this empty home.
I'm cold. Hours of worry. Why won't he come?

Leaping figure

When every touch you make seems marvellous and exhilarating you feel at last – this is it – this is the way you should paint…just trying to surprise yourself with a masterpiece.

Journals, 2nd April 1964

You leap into paint:
its scuffs and strokes and splashes –
gouache seems a caress on paper,
oils a sticky glut, ink and wash
thunder and cloud. They make a man
of you, this body of contradictions
standing barefoot by the easel.
You leap over naysayers, the obstructers,
your damned neurosis, foggy doubt.
You leap over courts of justice,
steeples in autumn villages,
your mother's grip, your lover's smothering.

You leap over banisters, gates, fences:
your father misses you – he even says so,
your brother walks back, lovers unshackle
you, bruises are kisses. You're naked
on Pagham beach again, days of sun –
waves lull courage against your ankles,
a gull dives to nip your fingers,
talent snatches your hand. You laugh
down failure's throat. All that matters
is the next nude, the open landscape –
bells clanging from every rooftop
your name your name your name.

Pond overgrown by trees

I feel like a stranded dinosaur...I look at my work – the result of some forty years' effort and hope – and theirs – the result of 5 or 6 at the most. And it's I who feel defeated.

Journals, 7th April 1964

Spears of leaves slice the water,
branches wavering
through a stranded pond,
one willow drowning.

Goldfish are lit cigarettes
hidden under a leaf.
Years defeat me,
yet I cling to this patchwork –
russet, sky, dank moss.

I could hold my breath here,
become that twig tapping
the pond's liquid cage –
while water spends hours
being cloud.

Figure with outstretched arms

*A critic once wrote that I seem to be obsessed with what it feels like to have
a body. He was right...I find it a constant baffling mystery – the duality of
I and myself.*

from 'Some notes on painting', August 1964

He stands, a mud-faced crucifix,
wide as a gate – his offered embrace.

I love you this much says the canvas,
arms open to touch the borders of myself.

He's merely a body – watch him spin
breath and fidgety blood.

Naked in the downpour, I surrender.
Rain stipples his skin, prickles

every hair – as if praise shivers
a wheatfield to wake my bones.

Group of bathers

The fountains were full of wet boys instead of water.

Journals, 1ˢᵗ January 1965

Love scorches me at its stem,
    this body a tower burning.
I hold him like drizzle through fingers,
        petals of flame.
My skin thickens to burnt umber –
    though I glisten the minute I paint.

You think it's simple making a man –
    rib or elbow, his navel, his heel.
Flesh is the texture of mud and I'm
God across every canvas, each dab
my oozy thumbprint, daubing indigo, ochre
    – what ecstasy of worms!

This peony flung onto water
becomes his throat the colour of snow,
    another lobe edged by magenta –
midnight's hollyhock, drenched and joyous –
a shout shimmered from fountains. The drops
    rainstorm their chests.

I long to launch their torsos into blue –
    watch them strive on Icarus wings,
my feathery heroes. I ache the moment I know
all that soaring gives way to plummet,
    when they plunge for my seasick arms
        and we drown in air.

Snowdrift at Harrow Hill (Ramsay McClure)

...to live with someone who excites pity and irritation – who mirrors all one's own failings with no counterbalancing virtues, except a mule-like patience and willingness to suffer.

Journals, 2nd May 1965

Snowed in like a drunken husband –
jumpy under his glare – I get it wrong.
Everything cracks: finest china,
light-bulbs, ice across the pond
where we swam and sank last summer.

Our country retreat. I want Paris again,
where he let us love and we glimmered
like a garden. Look at us now: blank
white inches on our roof, spindly
branches, a postage stamp of green.

I'm cut off, exiled here.
Icicles click between his teeth.
If a kiss can't survive like a crocus
let's bicker again – the best of enemies,
find the worst words to say and never part.

The trial

It is difficult to bear in mind that with all one's honours, distinctions,
successes etc one remains a member of the criminal class…How can one
feel part of one's time and society in that case.

Journals, July 18th 1965

Am I the hooded prisoner? Yellow ropes
bind me. My sorry neck tilts towards
the gunmetal warder, as if wary
of another punch. At the edge
of court, desire is a spearhead candle,
its lemon flame too weak to keep me warm.

How guilty am I? A tiny white
hole in my hood, peepshow to the jury.
I dream of a dozen louts tumbling,
if I'm lucky – their panther limbs
bristle as they nuzzle and nudge, lick
sweat from this man's nape, that man's lip.

May I say nothing? These words can
be used in evidence against me.
Self-snares pinion me like a verdict.
Blind my eyes. Justice feathers the air –
hooded and tied, cowed and irresistible.

Two figures by a pool

Symptoms of being in love; a slight feeling of inflation on the left side of the thorax, as though something were lodged there – some winged creature.

Journals, 9th August 1965

One man stirs deep water
with a stick, while another
steeps his shins, reaches away,
distracted, blue between them.

Poets are wrong – it's not my heart
afflicted. Feel the pliable surfaces
of skin: palms, thighs, belly
– here's his imprint

like stigmata, love's subtle cuts.
Have I swallowed a dragonfly?
Its wings chafe my ribcage.

So it goes with us – this dark pool
curdling, this struggle for flight.

Figures and trees

The making of a series of wet marks across the white board in a sequence of colours (blue black I fancy at the moment) and see where it leads.

Journals, 2nd July 1972

A green man – a blue man –

                    Have they something
to say to each other? Will trees overwhelm them?

I'll follow wherever they lead –

My hand's agitation   unknots   making its mark

Two wet blue flags   swish

                    below black
begin a conversation   on snow

Olive, sap and linden soak my fingertips –

                    This path of paint
evolves an improvisation of leaves

Standing figure, Kouros (Johnny Walsh)

*How does one report this? Johnny Walsh, with whom, in the past, I have
had more intense pleasure than any other person. I endured 40 minutes of
his presence & then made excuses.*

Journals, 7th March 1973

I wanted to be skinned alive – bumped
every poof's shoulder to reach him,
chest a box of frogs
when he stroked my stubble.

What d'you call that feeling?
Bollock-naked for hours in his studio,
he clocked me over & over, back
to the easel – dab dab with his brush.

In his picture my muscles are stripes
of shit & mustard, body
a shield, right hand a fist.
Look how vague he makes my face.

Now he wants me to piss off
out of it, hoick my whiff
& shoes off his carpet,
fizzle to nothing.

I should've asked him to say those
words again – *kouros* – *viridian* –
ultramarine. I never hear their noise
without missing his gift of the gab.

What did I mean to him? Whatever
it was, blown out like a match – kaput.
His lips puff a little O
& I'm Johnny Yesterday.

Two studies of a head

*...am ravished by the face of the boy Egyptian King Tutankamoun...The
only thing comparable is the dark-haired onyx-eyed butcher boy at the
Co-op who stood so patiently, with folded arms, on Saturday, waiting in
the queue to pay for three bars of Fry's Crunchie.*

Journals, 3rd November 1974

Peel off the pharaoh's gold-leaf mask,
unlace the butcher boy's apron –
what's left but two shivery lads?

Let me cover, uncover you.
I mean no harm, only to consider
that infinite understanding in your face.

Your eyes teach patience to an ageing fool.
Lift your chin for me. Tilt your head.
Love may wait and never be served.

Pharaohs have no need of queues.
Here's three chocolate honeycombs,
stolen and sticky in our brittle mouths.

Model seated on a blue cushion

No desire – only a desire for desire –

Journals, 13th April 1976

A blue cushion takes his weight.
He looks away to the lavender distance.
His spine nulls me.

Shoulder blades jut like wing stubs –
bricks in his back turn against me.
Wingless myself, I can't climb his wall.

Cancer has sliced and singed me.
My body's a bag of shit,
this feeble dangle between my legs

all fingers and thumbs. Pluck me,
but no song comes: dull thud
of strings – gut splinters, passion snapped.

Burning fields

I feel deeply shocked by the words –"will not recover".

Journals, 4th October 1976

I thought I'd race through meadows again,
but orange flags of damage
blacken my heels,
speckle ash on my tongue.

I thought I'd limp into another season
though trust in recovery sizzles,
snuffs my roots.

Stitches and sickness stain my acres
where soil speaks:

> *I've hosted seed,*
> *   arrowheads*
> *of jade –*
> *   copper-eared wheat*
> *healthy as harvest,*
> *   stunned by flame's*
> *last will and testament*
> *   I'm lost in it –*
> *soot and smoke*

Harrow Hill in March

Grey & drizzling with rain, but the trees are in bud & there is the
look, though not the feeling, of spring…The very idea of painting again
nauseates me. There is nothing I want to do except sleep. Oblivion.

Journals, 27th March 1977

Lilac sky with an absence
of cloud almost sustains me.

Lines fence me in against rain,
but the point of my roof

can't protect me. Life opens
one black window

where I'm calling goldfinches
sparrows and starlings,

even wanting a heron's grey cry –
anything to sing me to sleep.

I'll hang on to this green diagonal –
sloping grass lit between trees.

Still life with greengages and yellow cup

*I sit here sipping sherry, rocking in my chair & looking around the room
at the familiar bottles & boxes. Brushes hanging from the shelf and
standing up in jugs like dried out blossoms.*

Journals, 12th June 1977

     Where should I pour my days?
These brushes are cyclamens dropping,
water blanched from every sable hair.
     Nothing heals –
   not even that gap between
a sky-blue jug and three greengages,
though the twig, those sprigs of leaf,
      spurt their silver rumours.

Is love an apple rocking on a plate,
      plucked – uneaten – given up?
The plate's a puddle, the table divided.
Years ago I mixed and paced, smoked and painted,
     sailing my studio kingdom,
      my weathers of colour.

     Shall I drink now from the yellow cup,
let rainfall soak a broken lip
          a parchment tongue –
   stream into my hands until
I'm overflowing? Look how this slate
        edge balances green,
   how empty my hours have become –
like a jug loses purpose when the pouring's done.

Horizontal figure

I thought in bed last night about Boulanger. The French Canadian I picked up in the York Minster one night about 1944 & took him home to bed…He lay sleeping heavy with drink… Some weeks later…I was told he'd been blown to pieces on the Anzio Beachhead.

Journals, 8th September 1977

Adieu to the drowsy youth,
his arm flung back in dreams.
My kisses fail to wake him –
this skitter of moths across skin.

Thirty years gone, still warm
between sheets, I swim there again –
his nipples the sheen from oyster-shells,
his navel mother-of-pearl.

He is pebbles and breadcrumbs.
I can't cup his charred gifts
in my hand, or forget his eyes.

Elegiac landscape

9.30 a.m. The capsules have been taken with some whiskey…I cannot believe I have committed suicide since nothing has happened. No big bang or cut wrists. 65 was long enough for me. It wasn't a complete failure I did some good wor…

Journals, 4th November 1977 (last entry)

If sex is dead, art is dead.
I ditch the cancer era – fix my exit.
Leave me the company of words –
                          their black solace.

I'm raw sienna – rose madder – renaissance gold.
My bathers and wrestlers, my naked men
gather like silence beside me.

Watch me sift towards unfinished brushstrokes

        this bliss

                                this whiteout

        me   a figure walking

                into snow